30
MINUTES
OR LESS

Fresh
Food

30 | Fresh
MINUTES
OR LESS | Food

This is a Parragon Book

First published in 2006

Parragon

Queen Street House

4 Queen Street

Bath BA1 1HE, UK

ISBN: 1-40547-383-5

Printed in China

Produced by the Bridgewater Book Company Ltd

Front cover photography by Laurie Evans

Front cover home economy by Carol Tennant

Notes for the Reader

This book uses metric and imperial measurements. Follow the same units of measurement
throughout; do not mix metric and imperial. All spoon measurements are level: teaspoons are
assumed to be 5 ml, and tablespoons are assumed to be 15 ml. Unless otherwise stated,
milk is assumed to be full fat, eggs and individual vegetables are medium and pepper is
freshly ground black pepper.

Recipes using raw or very lightly cooked eggs should be avoided by children, the elderly,
pregnant women, convalescents and anyone suffering from an illness. Pregnant women and
breast-feeding women are advised to avoid eating peanuts and peanut products.

Contents

Introduction

This book is written for all those who enjoy eating good food but lack the time to spend hours in the kitchen. Cooking isn't rocket science nor is it only for the super-skilled – anyone with some fresh ingredients and a few pots and pans can produce something good to eat, and quickly, too. All the recipes in this book can be completed in 30 minutes or less.

Fast food is not just about burgers or baked beans on toast; fast food can mean a sliver of top-quality prosciutto wrapped around a slice of perfectly ripe melon. Fresh food makes fabulous fast food – and if you cook it as little as possible, you'll benefit from the maximum amount of nutrients that the ingredients possess.

The book is divided into four chapters: Snacks and Starters, Main Courses, Salads and Desserts, giving you the option of preparing simple meals for everyday eating or serving up a dinner party feast with the minimum of time and effort. Recipes have been inspired by regional cuisines from around the world, drawing on a wealth of flavours to excite your taste buds and satisfy your appetite.

CHOOSING FRESH FOOD

If you spend a little time selecting good quality ingredients, you'll really notice the difference on your plate. This doesn't mean you've always got to scour your local farmers' market for the best organic produce at a premium price – there's plenty of quality fresh food on offer at your local supermarket. The key to identifying truly fresh food is that it looks good and smells good, too. Here are a few pointers as to what to look for and how to store it:

Meat: meat should never be slimy nor should it smell. Exposed bones should be a pinkish-blue colour and any fat should be pale. If tightly wrapped, pierce the clingfilm and store in the bottom of the refrigerator for up to two days.

Dairy produce: milk and yogurt will keep if covered and refrigerated for about three days. Unsalted butter will keep for two weeks; salted for one month as long as it is refrigerated and tightly wrapped. The freshness of cheese depends on whether it's hard or soft and the ripeness of it when purchased. To keep at its best, wrap in clingfilm and remove from the refrigerator an hour before serving.

Fish: fish must be bought and consumed when it's still very fresh - it shouldn't smell and should have bright eyes, red gills and firm flesh. It's always best to buy fish off the slab rather than pre-packed. Your fishmonger will bone, scale, clean and fillet the fish for you if you don't fancy doing this yourself (it saves your time, too). Refrigerate and eat on the day of purchase.

Vegetables: always choose vegetables that are young and fresh. They should be brightly coloured, unwrinkled and unblemished. Unwrap anything that comes in cellophane and store in the salad compartment of the refrigerator or in a larder. If there is no room in the refrigerator, do not keep vegetables in your kitchen in polythene bags because they will sweat and rot.

Fruit: fruit should be bright-skinned and have a strong scent without being overpowering. Some fruit, such as pears, are rarely in perfect condition in the shops because they are only completely ripe for one day – they should therefore be bought in advance and ripened at home. Don't store soft fruit for more than two days in a refrigerator and do not prepare until ready for use. Citrus and hard fruit will stay fresh for a few weeks.

The recipes in this book are all based on fresh food, and there are no complicated cooking methods or elaborate presentations, nor will you need to use every pot and pan in the kitchen. Whether it's a simple Mixed Herb Omelette, a tasty Grilled Steak with Tomatoes and Garlic, a tangy Traditional Greek Salad or fragrant Baked Peaches, there's nothing to match the eating experience of real fresh food.

Chapter One
Snacks and Starters

Tomato Bread

5 minutes to the table

SERVES 4

ingredients

6-8 slices French bread or other
   crusty loaf
3-4 tomatoes, halved
1-2 garlic cloves, halved (optional)
extra-virgin olive oil, for drizzling
   (optional)

method

To prepare this at its simplest, rub the bread slices with the cut sides of
the tomato halves, letting the juice and seeds soak into the bread. If
the bread is too soft, you can lightly toast it beforehand.

   Other options are to flavour the bread slices with garlic by rubbing
with the garlic halves in the same way, or drizzle extra-virgin olive oil
over the top of the tomatoes.

variation

To make a more substantial snack, serve the bread with a plate of
thinly sliced serrano ham and Manchego cheese, and let guests
assemble open sandwiches for themselves.

Mixed Herb Omelette

15 minutes to the table

SERVES 1

ingredients

2 large eggs
2 tbsp milk
40 g/1½ oz butter
1 fresh flat-leaf parsley sprig,
    stem bruised
leaves from 1 fresh flat-leaf
    parsley sprig
1 fresh chervil sprig
2 fresh chives, chopped
salt and pepper

method

Break the eggs into a bowl. Add the milk and salt and pepper to taste, and quickly beat until just blended.

Heat a 20-cm/8-inch omelette pan or frying pan over a medium-high heat until very hot and you can feel the heat rising from the surface. Add 25 g/1 oz of the butter and use a fork to rub it over the base and around the side of the pan as it melts.

As soon as the butter stops sizzling, pour in the eggs. Shake the pan forwards and backwards over the heat and use the fork to stir the eggs around the pan in a circular motion. Do not scrape the base of the pan.

As the omelette begins to set, use the fork to push the cooked egg from the edge towards the centre, so that the remaining uncooked egg comes in contact with the hot base of the pan. Continue doing this for 3 minutes, or until the omelette looks set on the bottom but is still slightly runny on top.

Put the herbs in the centre of the omelette. Tilt the pan away from the handle, so that the omelette slides towards the edge of the pan. Use the fork to fold the top half of the omelette over the herbs. Slide the omelette onto a plate, then rub the remaining butter over the top. Serve immediately.

variation

For a more traditional omelette aux fines herbes, finely chop the parsley, chervil and some fresh tarragon leaves and snip the chives, then fold them into the egg and milk mixture before cooking.

Prawn Toasts
20 minutes to the table

method

Pound the prawns to a pulp in a mortar with a pestle or with the base of a cleaver.

Mix the prawns with one of the egg whites and half the cornflour in a bowl. Add the sugar and salt, and stir in the coriander. Mix the remaining egg white with the remaining cornflour in a jug.

Remove the crusts from the bread and cut each slice into 8 triangles. Brush the top of each piece with the egg white and cornflour mixture, then add 1 teaspoon of the prawn mixture and spread smoothly over the top.

Heat enough oil for deep-frying in a wok, deep-fat fryer or large, heavy-based saucepan until it reaches 180–190°C/350–375°F, or until a cube of bread browns in 30 seconds. Without overcrowding the pan, cook the toasts prawn-side up for 2 minutes. Turn and cook for a further 2 minutes until beginning to turn golden brown. Remove with a slotted spoon, drain on kitchen paper and keep warm in a low oven while cooking the remainder.

MAKES 16

ingredients

100 g/3½ oz raw prawns, peeled and deveined

2 egg whites

2 tbsp cornflour

½ tsp sugar

pinch of salt

2 tbsp finely chopped fresh coriander leaves

2 slices day-old white bread

vegetable or groundnut oil, for deep-frying

Soba Noodle Rolls
30 minutes to the table

MAKES 24

ingredients

115 g/4 oz sushi-grade tuna or piece of tuna fillet

1 tbsp oil

100 g/3½ oz soba noodles, broken into pieces

1 spring onion, green part only, thinly sliced

1 tbsp light soy sauce

½ tbsp rice vinegar

pinch of wasabi paste

1 tbsp pickled ginger, finely chopped

6 small sheets toasted nori

½ cucumber, peeled and finely shredded

method

If using a piece of tuna fillet, heat the oil in a frying pan and sear the tuna all over for 6 minutes, or until almost cooked through. Cut the sushi-grade tuna or cooked tuna into strips.

Meanwhile, cook the soba noodles in a saucepan of boiling water until just cooked through, drain and rinse under cold running water. Drain thoroughly. Gently mix the noodles with the spring onion, soy sauce, vinegar, wasabi and pickled ginger in a bowl.

Divide the noodle mixture into 6 equal portions. Put a sheet of nori shiny-side down on a rolling mat with the longest end towards you and mound a portion of the noodle mixture on the bottom third of the nori. Lay a sixth of the cucumber on top, then a layer of tuna strips.

To roll the sushi, fold the mat over, starting at the end where the ingredients are and tucking in the end of the nori to start the roll. Keep rolling, lifting up the mat as you go and keeping the pressure even but gentle until you have finished the roll. Moisten the top edge of the nori with water to seal the sushi roll closed. Don't worry if anything falls out of the sides – just push it back in.

Remove the roll from the mat and cut into 4 even-sized pieces with a wet, very sharp knife. Turn the pieces on end and arrange them on a plate. Repeat with the remaining ingredients.

cook's tip

Lay the bamboo rolling mat on a chopping board with bamboo strips going horizontally from you and place on plastic wrap before rolling.

Pear and Roquefort Open-face Sandwiches

15 minutes to the table

MAKES 4

ingredients

4 slices walnut bread, about
   1 cm/½ inch thick
4 thin slices cured ham, such as
   Bayonne or Parma ham
2 ripe pears, such as Conference,
   peeled, halved, cored and thinly
   sliced lengthways
100 g/3½ oz Roquefort cheese, very
   thinly sliced
mixed salad leaves, washed and dried,
   to serve

WALNUT VINAIGRETTE

125 ml/4 fl oz walnut oil
3 tbsp white wine vinegar or lemon
   juice
1 tsp Dijon mustard
½ tsp caster sugar
salt and pepper
2 tbsp chopped walnuts

method

To make the vinaigrette, put all ingredients in a jar, then blend using a stick blender until a thick emulsion forms. Alternatively, put all the ingredients in a screw-top jar, secure the lid and shake vigorously until the emulsion forms. Taste and adjust the seasoning if necessary.

Preheat the grill to high. Toast the bread slices on both sides under the preheated grill until crisp but not brown. Do not turn off the grill.

Fold or cut the ham slices to cover each slice of bread, then divide the pear slices equally between the bread slices. Lay the cheese slices on top.

Return the bread slices to the grill and cook until the cheese melts and bubbles. Mix the salad leaves with the walnut vinaigrette and serve 1 or 2 sandwiches per person with the salad on the side.

variations

Try these other open-face sandwich ideas. For a crunchy snack in a flash, spread slices of sourdough bread with salted butter and top with thinly sliced new-season radishes and a sprinkling of finely chopped fresh parsley. For a quick alternative to a traditional Croque Monsieur, top toasted bread slices with cooked ham and thin slices of Comté cheese, and grill until the cheese melts and bubbles. Spread thick slices of untoasted bread with salted butter and top with a selection of thinly sliced cooked or smoked sausages.

Steamed Spring Rolls
25 minutes to the table

method

Put the pancakes between 2 dampened tea towels and leave for 2 minutes until soft. Alternatively, soak them in warm water and lift out one at a time to work on. Meanwhile, cook the vermicelli noodles in a saucepan of boiling water until just cooked through, drain and rinse under cold running water. Drain thoroughly.

Put 1-2 basil leaves in the centre of a pancake and top with a little chilli sauce. Arrange 2 prawns on top and then some of the spring onions and carrot. Add a few noodles and roll up. Flip one edge of the pancake over the filling, fold the sides over to enclose and roll up. Repeat with the remaining pancakes and filling.

Arrange the filled pancakes in a single layer in the top of a steamer. Cook over simmering water for 4-5 minutes until heated through. Serve immediately with extra chilli sauce for dipping.

MAKES 12

ingredients

12 rice flour pancakes
55 g/2 oz rice vermicelli noodles
12-24 fresh Thai basil leaves
2 tbsp chilli sauce, plus extra
    for serving
24 cooked peeled tiger prawns
4 spring onions, cut into thin strips
1 carrot, cut into matchsticks

Grilled Aubergine with Halloumi and Tapenade

30 minutes to the table

SERVES 4

ingredients

1 large aubergine, thinly sliced
   lengthways

5 tbsp olive oil

70 g/2½ oz black olives, stoned

1 tbsp capers

2 tbsp chopped fresh flat-leaf parsley

50 g/1¾ oz sun-dried tomatoes in oil
   (drained weight)

2 garlic cloves

1 tsp lemon juice

175 g/6 oz halloumi cheese,
   cut into sticks

method

Preheat the oven to 220°C/425°F/Gas Mark 7. Brush the aubergine slices with 2 tablespoons of the oil and place on a baking sheet. Bake the aubergines in the preheated oven for 10 minutes until soft. Leave to cool.

Meanwhile, for the tapenade, put the olives, capers, half the parsley, the tomatoes and garlic in a food processor and pulse until roughly chopped, or roughly chop by hand. Add 2 tablespoons of the remaining oil and the lemon juice, then pulse again to form a smooth paste, or beat into the olive mixture by hand.

Preheat the grill to high. When the aubergines are cool enough to handle, spread each one with a little of the tapenade. Put a couple of the cheese sticks at the end of each aubergine slice, roll up and secure with a cocktail stick.

Brush the aubergine rolls with the remaining oil and cook under the preheated grill, turning once, until golden brown and the cheese is beginning to melt. Serve scattered with the remaining parsley.

Grilled Sardines with Lemon Sauce

30 minutes to the table

SERVES 4

ingredients

LEMON SAUCE
1 large lemon
50g/2oz unsalted butter
1 tbsp chopped fresh fennel leaves

25 g/1 oz unsalted butter
12 fresh sardines, cleaned, scaled
   (see cook's tip) and heads removed
salt and pepper

method

Peel the lemon. Using a small, serrated knife, remove all the white pith from the lemon. Cut between the membranes and ease out the flesh segments, discarding any pips. Chop finely and set aside.

Preheat the grill or barbecue. Melt 25 g/1 oz of the butter in a small saucepan and season to taste with salt and pepper. Brush the sardines all over with the melted butter and cook under the preheated grill or on the barbecue, turning once, for 5–6 minutes until cooked through.

Meanwhile, to make the sauce, melt the remaining butter in the saucepan, then remove from the heat. Stir in the chopped lemon and fennel.

Transfer the sardines to a warmed platter, pour the sauce over and serve immediately.

cook's tip

To clean the sardines, slit open the belly and remove the insides. Rinse and dry. To scale, hold each fish in turn by its tail under cold running water and run your hand along the body from tail to head until the scales are removed.

Baked Courgettes
20 minutes to the table

method

Preheat the oven to 200°C/400°F/Gas Mark 6.

Slice the courgettes lengthways into 4 strips each. Brush with oil and place on an ovenproof tray.

Bake the courgettes in the oven for 10 minutes without letting them get too floppy.

Remove the courgettes from the oven. Arrange slices of cheese on top and sprinkle with diced tomato and basil or oregano. Return to the oven for 5 minutes or until the cheese melts.

Remove the courgettes from the oven and transfer carefully to serving plates, or serve straight from the baking dish, garnished with fresh basil leaves.

SERVES 4

ingredients

4 medium courgettes

2 tbsp extra-virgin olive oil

115 g/4 oz mozzarella cheese, sliced thinly

2 large tomatoes, deseeded and diced

2 tsp fresh oregano or basil, chopped

a few fresh basil leaves, to garnish

Prosciutto with Rocket
10 minutes to the table

SERVES 4

ingredients

115 g/4 oz rocket
1 tbsp lemon juice
3 tbsp extra-virgin olive oil
225 g/8 oz thinly sliced prosciutto
salt and pepper

method

Wash the rocket in cold water and pat dry with kitchen paper. Put the leaves in a bowl.

Pour the lemon juice into a small bowl and season to taste with salt and pepper. Whisk in the oil, then pour the dressing over the rocket and toss lightly to coat.

Arrange the slices of prosciutto in folds on 4 individual serving plates, then divide the rocket equally between the plates. Serve at room temperature.

variations

For a more substantial salad, add 1 thinly sliced fennel bulb and 2 thinly sliced oranges to the rocket in the bowl at the beginning of the method. Substitute orange juice or balsamic vinegar for the lemon juice in the dressing.

Melon and Kiwi Fruit Bowl

10 minutes to the table

SERVES 2

ingredients

1 small Charentais, Cantaloupe or
   Galia melon

2 kiwi fruit

method

Cut the melon into quarters and remove and discard the seeds. Using a sharp knife, remove the melon flesh from the skin and cut into chunks. Put in a bowl.

Peel the kiwi fruit and cut the flesh into slices. Add to the melon and gently mix together. Cover and refrigerate until required or divide equally between 2 serving dishes and serve immediately.

Chapter Two
Main Courses

Chicken with Goat's Cheese and Basil

25 minutes to the table

SERVES 4

ingredients

4 skinless, boneless chicken breasts,
    about 115 g/4 oz each
100 g/3½ oz soft goat's cheese
small bunch of fresh basil, reserving
    sprigs for garnish
2 tbsp olive oil
salt and pepper

method

Using a sharp knife, slit along one long edge of each chicken breast, then carefully open out each breast to make a small pocket. Divide the goat's cheese equally between the pockets and tuck 3-4 basil leaves in each, leaving the sprigs in reserve for a garnish. Close the openings and season the chicken breasts to taste with salt and pepper.

Heat the oil in a large frying pan, add the chicken breasts and cook gently for 15-20 minutes, turning several times, until golden and tender, and the juices run clear when a skewer is inserted into the thickest part of the meat. Serve warm, garnished with a basil sprig.

Chicken and Shiitake Mushrooms

25 minutes to the table

SERVES 4

ingredients

MARINADE

175 g/6 oz sugar

225 ml/8 fl oz soy sauce

1 tsp Chinese five-spice powder

225 ml/8 fl oz sweet sherry

STIR-FRY

2 tbsp vegetable oil

675 g/1 lb 8 oz boneless chicken
  breast, skinned and cut into
  2.5-cm/1-inch chunks

1 tsp grated fresh root ginger

3 carrots, thinly sliced

2 onions, thinly sliced

100 g/3½ oz fresh beansprouts

225 g/8 oz shiitake mushrooms,
  thinly sliced

3 tbsp chopped fresh coriander

boiled noodles, to serve

method

Put all the marinade ingredients in a bowl, mix well and set aside until required.

Heat the oil in a preheated wok or large frying pan over a medium-high heat. Add the chicken and stir-fry for 2 minutes, then add the ginger and stir-fry for 1 minute. Add the marinade and cook, stirring, for a further 2 minutes.

Add the carrots, onions, beansprouts, mushrooms and coriander one at a time and stir-fry for 30 seconds after each addition.

Once the marinade has reduced and thickened, transfer the stir-fry to warmed serving bowls. Serve hot with boiled noodles.

Red Curry Pork with Peppers

25 minutes to the table

method

Heat the oil in a preheated wok or large frying pan over a medium-high heat. Add the onion and garlic and stir-fry for 1–2 minutes, or until soft but not brown.

Add the pork slices and stir-fry for 2–3 minutes until browned all over. Add the red pepper, mushrooms and curry paste.

Meanwhile, dissolve the coconut in a bowl of hot stock. Add to the pan with the soy sauce. Bring to the boil, then reduce the heat and simmer for 4–5 minutes until the liquid has reduced and thickened.

Add the tomatoes and coriander and cook, stirring, for 1–2 minutes before serving.

cook's tip

To peel tomatoes, cut a small cross in the base of each tomato with a sharp knife. Put in a heatproof bowl, cover with boiling water and leave for a minute or so. Remove with a slotted spoon and plunge into cold water. Drain and peel off the skins.

SERVES 4-6

ingredients

2 tbsp vegetable or groundnut oil

1 onion, roughly chopped

2 garlic cloves, chopped

450 g/1 lb pork fillet, thickly sliced

1 red pepper, deseeded and
    cut into squares

175 g/6 oz mushrooms, quartered

2 tbsp red Thai curry paste

115 g/4 oz creamed coconut, chopped

300 ml/10 fl oz hot pork
    or vegetable stock

2 tbsp Thai soy sauce

4 tomatoes, peeled (see cook's tip),
    deseeded and chopped

handful of fresh coriander, chopped

Surf 'n' Turf Skewers
25 minutes to the table

SERVES 2

ingredients

225 g/8 oz fillet steak,
   about 2.5 cm/1 inch thick
8 raw tiger prawns, peeled and
   deveined
olive oil, for oiling
55 g/2 oz butter
2 garlic cloves, crushed
3 tbsp chopped fresh parsley, plus
   extra sprigs to garnish
finely grated rind and juice of 1 lime
salt and pepper
lime wedges, to garnish
crusty bread, to serve

method

Cut the steak into 2.5-cm/1-inch cubes.

Thread an equal number of the steak cubes and prawns onto 4 oiled flat metal kebab skewers or presoaked wooden skewers. Season the kebabs to taste with pepper.

Preheat the grill to medium. Meanwhile, put half the butter and garlic in a small saucepan and heat gently until melted. Remove from the heat and add half the parsley, lime rind and juice and salt and pepper to taste.

Brush the kebabs with some of the flavoured butter. Put the kebabs on an oiled grill rack and cook under the preheated grill for 4-8 minutes until the steak is cooked according to your taste and the prawns turn pink, turning the kebabs frequently during cooking and brushing with the remaining flavoured butter halfway through cooking.

Meanwhile, melt the remaining butter with the garlic in a separate small saucepan, remove from the heat and add the remaining parsley and lime rind and juice with salt and pepper to taste. Serve the kebabs hot on the skewers, with the flavoured butter spooned over. Garnish with lime wedges and parsley sprigs, and serve with crusty bread to mop up the buttery juices.

Griddled Steak with Tomatoes and Garlic

25 minutes to the table

SERVES 4

ingredients

3 tbsp olive oil, plus extra
    for brushing
700 g/1 lb 9 oz tomatoes, peeled
    (see cook's tip) and chopped
1 red pepper, deseeded and chopped
1 onion, chopped
2 garlic cloves, finely chopped
1 tbsp chopped fresh flat-leaf parsley
1 tsp dried oregano
1 tsp sugar
4 entrecôte or rump steaks, about
    175 g/6 oz each
salt and pepper

method

Put the oil, tomatoes, red pepper, onion, garlic, parsley, oregano and sugar in a heavy-based saucepan and season to taste with salt and pepper. Bring to the boil, then reduce the heat and simmer, uncovered, for 15 minutes.

Meanwhile, preheat a griddle pan over a high heat. Snip any fat around the outsides of the steaks. Season each generously with pepper (no salt) and brush with oil. When the griddle pan is very hot, add the steaks and cook for 1 minute on each side. Reduce the heat to medium and cook according to taste: 1½–2 minutes on each side for rare; 2½–3 minutes on each side for medium; or 3–4 minutes on each side for well done.

Transfer the steaks to warmed individual plates and spoon the sauce over. Serve immediately.

cook's tip

To peel tomatoes, cut a small cross in the base of each tomato with a sharp knife. Put in a heatproof bowl, cover with boiling water and leave for a minute or so. Remove with a slotted spoon and plunge into cold water. Drain and peel off the skins.

Mussels with Fennel
25 minutes to the table

method

Heat the oil in a large, heavy-based saucepan or stockpot over a medium-high heat. Add the onions and fennel and cook, stirring, for 3 minutes. Add the garlic and cook, stirring, for a further 2 minutes, or until the onions and fennel are soft but not brown.

Add the wine and sherry and leave to bubble until reduced by half. Add the tomatoes with their juices and bring to the boil, stirring. Add the sugar and salt and pepper to taste, reduce the heat and simmer, uncovered, for 5 minutes.

Meanwhile, clean the mussels by scrubbing or scraping the shells and pulling out any beards that are attached to them. Discard any with broken shells or any that refuse to close when tapped.

Reduce the heat under the saucepan to very low. Add the mussels, cover and simmer, shaking the saucepan frequently, for 4 minutes until the mussels are opened. Discard any mussels that remain closed. Remove the remaining mussels from the saucepan and divide between 4 serving bowls. Re-cover the saucepan and simmer for a further minute.

Stir the parsley into the juices in the saucepan. Taste and adjust the seasoning. Pour the juices over the bowls of mussels, and serve immediately with plenty of bread for mopping up the juices.

SERVES 4-6

ingredients

4 tbsp olive oil

2 large onions, thinly sliced

1 fennel bulb, thinly sliced

2 large garlic cloves, finely chopped

350 ml/12 fl oz dry white wine

100 ml/3½ fl oz fino sherry

400 g/14 oz canned tomatoes

pinch of sugar

2 kg/4 lb 8 oz live mussels

handful of finely chopped fresh parsley

salt and pepper

crusty bread, to serve

Salmon with Watercress Cream

25 minutes to the table

SERVES 4

ingredients

25 g/1 oz unsalted butter

1 tbsp sunflower oil

4 salmon fillets, about 175 g/6 oz
   each, skinned

SAUCE

300 ml/10 fl oz crème fraîche

2 tbsp snipped fresh dill

1 garlic clove, finely chopped

100 ml/3½ fl oz dry white wine

bunch of watercress, a few sprigs
   reserved to garnish, finely chopped

salt and pepper

method

For the sauce, pour the crème fraîche into a large, heavy-based saucepan and heat gently to simmering point. Remove from the heat, stir in the dill and set aside until required.

Meanwhile, preheat a low oven. Melt the butter with the oil in a heavy-based frying pan. Add the salmon fillets and cook over a medium heat for 4–5 minutes on each side, or until cooked through. Remove the fish from the frying pan, cover and keep warm in a low oven.

Add the garlic to the frying pan and cook, stirring, for 1 minute. Pour in the wine, bring to the boil and cook until reduced. Stir the crème fraîche mixture into the frying pan and cook for 2–3 minutes, or until thickened.

Stir in the watercress and cook until just wilted. Season to taste with salt and pepper. Put the salmon fillets on warmed serving plates, spoon the watercress sauce over, garnish with the reserved watercress sprigs and serve immediately.

variation

If watercress is unavailable, then replace with the same amount of rocket or baby spinach leaves.

Italian Sardines
30 minutes to the table

SERVES 4

ingredients

1 tbsp olive oil

4 garlic cloves, roughly chopped

650 g/1 lb 7 oz fresh sardines,
    cleaned and scaled (see cook's tip)

grated rind of 2 lemons

2 tbsp chopped fresh
    flat-leaf parsley

salt and pepper

tomato, onion and chive salad,
    to serve

BRUSCHETTA

4 thick slices ciabatta or
    other rustic bread

2 garlic cloves, halved

2 large tomatoes, halved

method

Preheat the grill to medium. Heat the oil in a large, heavy-based frying pan. Add the chopped garlic and cook over a low heat, stirring frequently, until soft. For the bruschetta, lightly toast the bread on both sides under the preheated grill. Keep warm in a low oven.

Add the sardines to the frying pan and cook for 5 minutes, turning once. Sprinkle with the lemon rind and parsley and season to taste with salt and pepper.

Meanwhile, to finish the bruschetta, rub one side of each slice of toast with the cut side of a garlic clove half, then with the cut side of a tomato half. Divide the bruschetta and sardines between 4 serving plates and serve immediately with a tomato, onion and chive salad.

cook's tip

To clean the sardines, slit open the belly and remove the insides. Rinse and dry. To scale, hold each fish in turn by its tail under cold running water and run your hand along the body from tail to head until the scales are removed.

Grilled Red Mullet with Fennel and Peppers

25 minutes to the table

method

Pick over the mullet fillets and use a pair of tweezers to remove the fine bones running down the centre of each fillet.

Heat half the oil in a large sauté or frying pan with a tight-fitting lid over a medium-high heat. Add the red peppers, fennel and garlic and stir well. Add salt and pepper to taste, then reduce the heat to medium-low, cover and cook for 15–20 minutes until soft.

Meanwhile, preheat the grill to high. When the grill is very, very hot, brush the skin of the fillets with some of the remaining oil and season to taste with salt and pepper. Put the fillets on a baking tray skin-side up, and cook under the preheated grill for 3 minutes, or until the skin crisps and turns golden brown.

Turn the fillets over, brush again with the remaining oil and season to taste with salt and pepper. Cook for a further minute or so until the flesh flakes easily when tested with the tip of a knife.

Divide the fennel and peppers equally between 4 plates. Cut each fillet in half and arrange 3 pieces on top of each portion of vegetables. Serve immediately with lemon wedges for squeezing over, if you like.

cook's tip

To avoid the messy business of removing the fine bones from the fish and to save time, ask your fish supplier to do it for you.

SERVES 4

ingredients

6 red mullet fillets, about 125 g/4½ oz each, scaled (see cook's tip)

4 tbsp olive oil

2 large red peppers, deseeded and thinly sliced

2 fennel bulbs, thinly sliced

2 large garlic cloves, crushed

salt and pepper

lemon wedges, to serve (optional)

Fusilli with Gorgonzola and Mushroom Sauce
20 minutes to the table

SERVES 4

ingredients

350 g/12 oz dried fusilli

3 tbsp olive oil

350 g/12 oz wild mushrooms (see
   cook's tip), sliced

1 garlic clove, finely chopped

400 ml/14 fl oz double cream

250 g/9 oz Gorgonzola cheese,
   crumbled

salt and pepper

2 tbsp chopped fresh flat-leaf parsley,
   to garnish

method

Bring a large saucepan of lightly salted water to the boil. Add the pasta, return to the boil and cook according to the packet instructions until tender but still firm to the bite.

Meanwhile, heat the oil in a large, heavy-based saucepan over a low heat. Add the mushrooms and cook, stirring frequently, for 5 minutes. Add the garlic and cook, stirring, for a further 2 minutes.

Add the cream, bring to the boil and cook for 1 minute until slightly thickened. Stir in the cheese and cook over a low heat until it has melted. Do not allow the sauce to boil once the cheese has been added. Season to taste with salt and pepper and remove from the heat.

Drain the pasta and add to the sauce. Toss well to coat, then serve immediately, garnished with the parsley.

cook's tip

Wild mushrooms have a much earthier flavour than cultivated ones, so they complement the strong taste of the cheese. Porcini are especially delicious, but rather expensive. Field or Caesar's mushrooms, if you can find them, would also be a good choice. Otherwise, use cultivated mushrooms, but add 25 g/1 oz dried porcini, presoaked for 20 minutes in 225 ml/8 fl oz hot water.

Vermicelli with Vegetable Ribbons

20 minutes to the table

SERVES 4

ingredients

350 g/12 oz dried vermicelli

3 carrots

3 courgettes

25 g/1 oz unsalted butter

1 tbsp olive oil

2 garlic cloves, finely chopped

85 g/3 oz fresh basil, shredded

25 g/1 oz fresh chives, finely snipped

25 g/1 oz fresh flat-leaf parsley, finely
   chopped

1 small head of radicchio, leaves
   shredded

salt and pepper

method

Bring a large saucepan of lightly salted water to the boil. Add the pasta, return to the boil and cook according to the packet instructions until tender but still firm to the bite.

Meanwhile, using a swivel-bladed vegetable peeler or a mandoline (see cook's tip) cut the courgettes and carrots into very thin strips. Melt the butter with the oil in a heavy-based frying pan. Add the carrot strips and garlic and cook over a low heat, stirring occasionally, for 5 minutes. Add the courgette strips and all the herbs and season to taste with salt and pepper.

Drain the pasta and add to the frying pan. Toss well to mix and cook briefly, stirring. Transfer to a warmed serving dish. Add the radicchio, toss well and serve immediately.

variation

If you like, you can garnish the dish with thin fresh shavings of Parmesan cheese or crumbled feta cheese.

cook's tip

A mandoline is a cookery gadget that predates the food processor and chops and slices with ease. It usually has adjustable blades and allows cutting to shapes such as thin slices, matchsticks or strands.

Sweet-and-Sour Vegetables with Cashew Nuts

20 minutes to the table

method

Heat both the oils in a preheated wok or large frying pan over a high heat. Add the onions and stir-fry for 1–2 minutes until beginning to soften.

Add the carrots, courgettes and broccoli and stir-fry for 2–3 minutes. Add the mushrooms, pak choi, sugar, soy sauce and vinegar and stir-fry for 1–2 minutes.

Meanwhile, toast the cashew nuts in a dry frying pan. Sprinkle over the stir-fry and serve immediately.

SERVES 4

ingredients

1 tbsp vegetable or groundnut oil

1 tsp chilli oil

2 onions, sliced

2 carrots, thinly sliced

2 courgettes, thinly sliced

115 g/4 oz broccoli, cut into florets

115 g/4 oz button mushrooms, sliced

115 g/4 oz small pak choi, halved

2 tbsp palm sugar or soft light brown sugar

2 tbsp Thai soy sauce

1 tbsp rice vinegar

55 g/2 oz raw unsalted cashew nuts

Chapter Three
Salads

Salad of Greens with Lemon Dressing
10 minutes to the table

method

Wash the salad leaves in cold water and discard any thick stems. Pat dry with kitchen paper and put in a salad bowl. Add the herbs.

Make the dressing by whisking the oil, lemon juice, garlic and salt and pepper to taste together in a small bowl. Taste and add more oil or lemon juice if necessary.

Just before serving, whisk the dressing, pour over the salad leaves and toss together. Serve immediately.

SERVES 4

ingredients

200 g/7 oz mixed baby salad leaves, such as corn salad, spinach, watercress and rocket

4 tbsp mixed chopped fresh herbs, such as flat-leaf parsley, mint, coriander and basil

about 4 tbsp extra-virgin olive oil

juice of about ½ lemon

1 garlic clove, crushed

salt and pepper

Traditional Greek Salad
15 minutes to the table

SERVES 4

ingredients

6 tbsp extra-virgin olive oil

2 tbsp freshly squeezed lemon juice

1 garlic clove, crushed

pinch of sugar

200 g/7 oz authentic Greek feta
    cheese (drained weight)

½ head iceberg lettuce or 1 lettuce
    such as Cos or escarole, shredded
    or sliced

4 tomatoes, quartered

½ cucumber, sliced

12 Greek black olives

2 tbsp chopped fresh herbs, such as
    oregano, flat-leaf parsley, mint or
    basil

salt and pepper

method

Make the dressing by whisking the oil, lemon juice, garlic, sugar and salt and pepper to taste together in a small bowl. Set aside until required.

Cut the feta cheese into 2.5-cm/1-inch cubes. Put the lettuce, tomatoes and cucumber in a salad bowl. Scatter over the cheese and toss together.

Just before serving, whisk the dressing, pour over the salad leaves and toss together. Scatter the olives with chopped herbs and serve immediately.

Lamb's Lettuce and Beetroot Salad

10 minutes to the table

SERVES 4

ingredients

175 g/6 oz lamb's lettuce
4 small cooked beetroot, diced
2 tbsp chopped walnuts

DRESSING
2 tbsp freshly squeezed lemon juice
2 garlic cloves, finely chopped
1 tbsp Dijon mustard
pinch of sugar
125 ml/4 fl oz sunflower oil
125 ml/4 fl oz soured cream
salt and pepper

method

Make the dressing by whisking the lemon juice, garlic, mustard, sugar and salt and pepper to taste together in a bowl. Gradually whisk in the oil. Lightly beat the soured cream, then whisk it into the dressing.

Put the lamb's lettuce in a bowl and pour over one-third of the dressing. Toss to coat.

Divide the lettuce equally between 4 individual bowls. Top each portion with an equal quantity of beetroot and drizzle with the remaining dressing. Sprinkle with the walnuts and serve immediately.

cook's tip

You can prepare the dressing in advance, but do not add it to the salad until you are ready to serve, otherwise the leaves will become soggy.

Julienne Vegetable Salad

20 minutes to the table

method

Preheat a low oven. Heat the oil in a preheated wok or large frying pan over a high heat. Add the tofu cubes and stir-fry for 3–4 minutes until browned all over. Remove with a slotted spoon, drain on kitchen paper and keep warm in a low oven.

Add the red onion and spring onions, garlic and carrots to the pan and stir-fry for 1–2 minutes. Add all the remaining vegetables, except the beansprouts, and stir-fry for 2–3 minutes. Add the beansprouts, then stir in the curry paste, soy sauce, vinegar, sugar and basil leaves and cook, stirring, for 30 seconds.

Meanwhile, soak the noodles in a heatproof bowl or saucepan of boiling water or stock for 2–3 minutes, or according to the packet instructions, until tender. Drain well.

Divide the noodles equally between 4 individual bowls. Pile the vegetables onto the noodles and top with the tofu cubes. Garnish with extra basil, if you like, and serve immediately.

SERVES 4

ingredients

4 tbsp vegetable or groundnut oil
225 g/8 oz tofu with herbs (drained weight), cubed
1 red onion, sliced
4 spring onions, cut into 5-cm/2-inch lengths
1 garlic clove, chopped
2 carrots, cut into matchsticks
115 g/4 oz fine French beans, trimmed
1 yellow pepper, deseeded and cut into strips
115 g/4 oz broccoli, cut into florets
1 large courgette, cut into matchsticks
55 g/2 oz fresh beansprouts
2 tbsp red Thai curry paste
4 tbsp Thai soy sauce
1 tbsp rice vinegar
1 tsp palm sugar or soft light brown sugar
few fresh Thai basil leaves, plus extra to garnish (optional)
350 g/12 oz rice vermicelli noodles

Raspberry and Feta Salad with Couscous

20 minutes to the table

SERVES 6

ingredients

350 g/12 oz couscous

600 ml/1 pint boiling chicken stock or
vegetable stock

350 g/12 oz fresh raspberries

225 g/8 oz feta cheese (drained
weight), cubed or crumbled

2 courgettes, thinly sliced

4 spring onions, diagonally sliced

55 g/2 oz pine kernels, toasted

small bunch of fresh basil, shredded

grated rind of 1 lemon

DRESSING

1 tbsp white wine vinegar

1 tbsp balsamic vinegar

4 tbsp extra-virgin olive oil

juice of 1 lemon

salt and pepper

method

Put the couscous in a large, heatproof bowl and pour over the stock. Stir well, cover and leave to soak until all the stock has been absorbed.

Meanwhile, pick over the raspberries, discarding any that are overripe.

Transfer the couscous to a large serving bowl and stir well to break up any lumps. Add the feta cheese, courgettes, spring onions, raspberries and pine kernels. Stir in the shredded basil and lemon rind and gently toss all the ingredients together.

Put all the dressing ingredients in a screw-top jar, with salt and pepper to taste, screw on the lid and shake until well blended. Pour over the salad and serve immediately.

Tabbouleh

25 minutes to the table

SERVES 4

ingredients

175 g/6 oz quinoa

600 ml/1 pint water

10 vine-ripened cherry tomatoes,
    deseeded and chopped

7.5-cm/3-inch piece cucumber, diced

3 spring onions, finely chopped

juice of ½ lemon

2 tbsp extra virgin olive oil

4 tbsp chopped fresh mint

4 tbsp chopped fresh coriander

4 tbsp chopped fresh parsley

salt and pepper

method

Put the quinoa in a medium-sized saucepan and cover with the water. Bring to the boil, then reduce the heat, cover and simmer over a low heat for 15 minutes. Drain if necessary.

Leave the quinoa to cool slightly before combining with the remaining ingredients in a salad bowl. Season to taste with salt and pepper. Serve at room temperature.

variation

The super-nutritious grain quinoa is featured in this version of tabbouleh, but the more traditional bulgar wheat or couscous can be used instead.

Orange and Fennel Salad

20 minutes to the table

method

Finely grate the rind from the oranges into a bowl and set aside. Using a small, serrated knife and working over a bowl to catch the juice, remove all the white pith from the oranges. Cut the oranges horizontally into thin slices.

Toss the orange slices with the fennel and onion slices in a salad bowl. Whisk the oil into the reserved orange juice, then spoon over the salad. Scatter the olive slices over the top, add the chilli, if using, then sprinkle with the orange rind. Garnish with parsley and serve immediately with French bread.

variations

Garnet-red blood oranges look stunning in this salad. Juicy dark grapes make an interesting alternative to the olives.

SERVES 4

ingredients

4 large juicy oranges
1 large fennel bulb, very thinly sliced
1 mild white onion, thinly sliced
2 tbsp extra-virgin olive oil
12 plump black olives, stoned and
    thinly sliced
1 fresh red chilli, deseeded and very
    thinly sliced (optional)
finely chopped fresh parsley,
    to garnish
French bread, to serve

Spinach and Garlic Salad

25 minutes to the table

SERVES 4

ingredients

12 garlic cloves, unpeeled

4 tbsp olive oil

450 g/1 lb baby spinach leaves,
    washed and dried

55 g/2 oz chopped walnuts or
    pine kernels

2 tbsp freshly squeezed lemon juice

salt and pepper

method

Preheat the oven to 190°C/375°F/Gas Mark 5. Put the garlic cloves in an ovenproof dish, add half the oil and toss to coat. Roast in the preheated oven for 15 minutes.

Transfer the garlic and oil to a salad bowl. Add the spinach leaves, walnuts, lemon juice and remaining oil. Toss well together and season to taste with salt and pepper.

Transfer the salad to individual dishes and serve immediately, while the garlic is still warm. Diners squeeze the softened garlic out of the skins at the table.

variation

Substitute young sorrel leaves for the baby spinach leaves to give this salad a delicious lemony flavour.

Chapter Four
Desserts

Grilled Honeyed Figs with Sabayon

15 minutes to the table

SERVES 4

ingredients

8 ripe fresh figs, halved

4 tbsp clear honey

leaves from 2 fresh rosemary sprigs,
   finely chopped (optional)

3 eggs

method

Preheat the grill to high. Arrange the figs, cut-side up, on the grill rack. Brush with half the honey and scatter over the rosemary, if using.

Cook under the preheated grill for 5–6 minutes, or until just beginning to caramelize.

Meanwhile, to make the sabayon, lightly whisk the eggs with the remaining honey in a large, heatproof bowl, then set over a saucepan of simmering water. Using a hand-held electric whisk, beat the eggs and honey together for 10 minutes, or until pale and thick.

Put 4 fig halves on each of 4 serving plates, add a generous spoonful of the sabayon and serve immediately.

caution

Recipes using raw or lightly cooked eggs should be avoided by infants, the elderly, pregnant women, convalescents and anyone suffering from an illness.

Griddled Bananas
20 minutes to the table

SERVES 4

ingredients
55 g/2 oz creamed coconut, chopped
150 ml/5 fl oz double cream
4 bananas
juice and finely grated rind of 1 lime,
   plus 1 lime, cut into wedges
1 tbsp vegetable or groundnut oil
50 g/1¾ oz desiccated coconut

method
Put the creamed coconut and cream in a small saucepan and heat over a low heat until the coconut has dissolved. Remove from the heat and leave to cool for 10 minutes, then whisk until thick but floppy.

Preheat a griddle pan over a high heat. Peel the bananas and toss in the lime juice and rind. Brush the preheated griddle pan with the oil, add the bananas and cook, turning once, for 2–3 minutes until soft and brown. Add the lime wedges halfway through the cooking time.

Meanwhile, preheat the grill to medium. Toast the desiccated coconut on a piece of foil under the preheated grill until lightly browned. Serve the bananas with the lime wedges and coconut cream, sprinkled with the coconut.

Nectarine Crunch

10 minutes to the table

method

Using a sharp knife, cut the nectarines in half, then remove and discard the stones. Chop the flesh into bite-sized pieces. Reserve a few pieces for decoration and put a few of the remaining pieces in the bottom of 3 sundae glasses. Put a layer of oat cereal in each glass, then drizzle over a little of the yogurt.

Put the jam and peach nectar in a large jug and stir together to mix. Add a few more nectarine pieces to the glasses and drizzle over a little of the jam mixture. Continue building up the layers in this way, finishing with a layer of yogurt and a sprinkling of oat cereal. Decorate with the reserved nectarine pieces and serve.

cook's tip

There is no need to peel the nectarines - just wash and pat dry with kitchen paper.

SERVES 3

ingredients

4 nectarines
175 g/6 oz raisin and nut crunchy
   oat cereal
300 ml/10 fl oz low-fat natural yogurt
2 tbsp peach jam
2 tbsp peach nectar

Mixed Fruit Brûlées

20 minutes to the table

SERVES 4

ingredients

450 g/1 lb prepared assorted summer
   fruit, such as strawberries,
   raspberries, blackcurrants,
   redcurrants and cherries, thawed
   if frozen
150 ml/5 fl oz soured cream
150 ml/5 fl oz low-fat natural
   fromage frais
1 tsp vanilla extract
4 tbsp demerara sugar

method

Preheat the grill to medium. Divide the prepared fruit equally between
4 small ramekin dishes.

   Combine the soured cream, fromage frais and vanilla extract in a
bowl. Spoon the mixture over the fruit to cover it completely.

   Top each serving with 1 tablespoon of demerara sugar. Cook the
desserts under the preheated grill until the sugar is beginning to
caramelize. Set aside for a couple of minutes before serving.

variations

For a richer result, use lightly whipped full-fat or half-fat single
or double cream instead of the soured cream and fromage frais.
Alternatively, for an even lower-fat version, use all fromage frais.

Baked Peaches
20 minutes to the table

SERVES 4

ingredients

4 large ripe fresh peaches
25 g/1 oz dried apricots, finely
    chopped
25 g/1 oz fresh blueberries
1 tbsp flaked almonds, toasted
2 tbsp medium sherry or orange juice
low-fat fromage frais or frozen yogurt,
    to serve

method

Preheat the oven to 180°C/350°F/Gas Mark 4.

If preferred, peel the peaches. To do this, cut a small cross in the base of each peach with a sharp knife. Put in a large, heatproof bowl, cover with boiling water and leave for 2 minutes. Remove with a slotted spoon and plunge into cold water. Drain and peel off the skins.

Cut the peaches in half and remove and discard the stones.

Put in an ovenproof dish with the peach stone cavity facing up.

Put the apricots in a bowl with the blueberries and stir together. Divide the fruit mixture equally between the peach stone cavities. Sprinkle with the almonds.

Pour over the sherry, then bake in the preheated oven for 10 minutes, or until heated through. Serve with fromage frais or frozen yogurt.

Peaches with Raspberry Sauce

20 minutes to the table

method

Purée the raspberries in a food processor or blender, then press through a fine non-metallic sieve into a bowl to remove the seeds.

Stir the orange rind and juice and liqueur into the raspberry purée. Add sugar to taste, stirring until the sugar dissolves. Cover and leave to chill in the refrigerator until required.

Peel the peaches. To do this, cut a small cross in the base of each peach with a sharp knife. Put in a large, heatproof bowl, cover with boiling water and leave for 2 minutes. Remove with a slotted spoon and plunge into cold water. Drain and peel off the skins. Cut the peaches in half and discard the stones.

Cut each peach half into quarters and stir into the raspberry sauce. Cover and leave to chill in the refrigerator until required.

When ready to serve, put 1-2 scoops of ice cream into individual glasses or bowls, then top with the peaches and spoon some extra sauce over. Serve with biscuits on the side, if you like.

cook's tip

When fresh raspberries are not in season, use frozen ones.

SERVES 4-6

ingredients

450 g/1 lb fresh raspberries (see cook's tip)
finely grated rind of 1 orange
2 tbsp freshly squeezed orange juice
2 tbsp Grand Marnier, Cointreau or other orange-flavoured liqueur
2-3 tbsp caster sugar
6 ripe fresh peaches

TO SERVE
vanilla ice cream
langues de chat biscuits (optional)

Grilled Cinnamon Oranges

10 minutes to the table

SERVES 6

ingredients

4 large oranges

1 tsp ground cinnamon

1 tbsp demerara sugar

method

Preheat the grill to high. Cut the oranges in half and discard any pips. Using a sharp or curved grapefruit knife, carefully cut the flesh away from the skin by cutting around the edge of the fruit. Cut across the segments to loosen the flesh into bite-sized pieces that will then spoon out easily.

Arrange the orange halves, cut-side up, in a shallow, flameproof dish. Mix the cinnamon with the sugar in a small bowl and sprinkle evenly over the orange halves.

Cook under the preheated grill for 3–5 minutes, or until the sugar has caramelized and is golden and bubbling. Serve immediately.

Index